GW00937880

fourteen poems

Issue 10

First published in 2023 by Fourteen Publishing.
fourteenpoems.com

Edited by Ben Townley-Canning.

Design and typeset by Stromberg Design.
strombergdesign.co.uk

Proofreading and copy editing by Lara Kavanagh.
lk-copy.com

Printed by Print2Demand Ltd, Westoning, Bedfordshire, UK.

ISBN:
978-1-7391697-3-2

Hello.

Welcome to the tenth issue of *fourteen poems*!

It's mind-blowing that we're here, to be honest. Launching *fourteen poems* back in 2019, I wasn't sure if anyone else would be as excited about queer contemporary poetry. I'm so pleased that you're all on board with me.

The thing I'm most proud of is the number of poets we've hopefully shone a light on. It's amazing to think that we've now published 140 poets, many for the first time in their careers. It's so exciting watching them go on to get published elsewhere and start bringing out their own pamphlets and collections. I love it so much.

This issue is no different, of course. As well as award-winning writers, regularly published poetry stars and some of my favourite names on the scene, I'm so pleased that we're also publishing new poets in these pages. I'm especially excited by Jesse Ogbeide's romantic, yearning poem 'watching men walk from the library window, thinking about love', David McGovern's rethinking of self care through hook-ups in 'The Bath Salts', and Lara Mae Simpson's sexy, thrilling 'Portrait of My Lover as a Leather Jacket'. Have a read of them and let me know what you think by emailing me at hello@14poems.com

I hope you find poems to love in this issue! If this is your first time reading us and you'd like to grab some back issues – or subscribe to future ones – head over to fourteenpoems.com/shop and have a look. There's a 40% discount for you as well – just use the code QUEERBOOKS at checkout.

Thanks for reading!

Ben Townley-Canning
Editor

Instagram:@14poems
Twitter: @fourteenpoems

contents:

Luke Worthy is a poet and fiction writer originally from Sheffield, UK now based in Amsterdam, The Netherlands. His work has been published in *Poetry Wales*, *Youth Word Up*, *Surfing the Twilight* (2019), and *Dear Life* (2022) among others. He was shortlisted for the 2021 New Poets Prize and has been commissioned to write a piece of children's literature for the cultural festival Leeds 2023. Luke is an alumnus of Sheffield Young Writers and a member of Hive Poetry.

Instagram: @worthyadventures

Twitter: @lukeworthy11

I Want the Assertiveness of

After Raymond Antrobus

erect nipples. The £ sign on every receipt,
every bill. The lactose running through your bowels.
The taxi drivers in Tenerife in a standoff of beeps.
The slip of a knife through a mushroom. Of a wave
sweeping up shingle and hurtling it at windows.
The needle that pierces the first stitch. Nightfall
after the solstice, the splatter of relish on your mash.
Of the scooter boys at Febo, the first flash of light
after the thunder cracks. The first piece of glass
that ever smashed. Of Kim Woodburn, escorted
away by Big Brother security guards.
Of the bike bell of a soon-to-clock-off Uber cyclist.
The whiff of spring onions shooting skywards
in the Amsterdam Bos. Of Lynx Africa,
of traffic lights without amber. Of Beyoncé
strutting the stage, Crazy in Love, of the way
I reached up, took hold of her hand.

Luke Worthy

Jaime Lock is a transmasc poet from the Isles of Scilly now living in North London, UK. They have poems in *Impossible Archetype*, *Signal House Edition*, and the anthology *Cornish Modern Poetries* (Broken Sleep Books, 2022), among others. They also sing sea shanties.

Instagram: @jfranceslock

Twitter: @jfranceslock

Urinals in the Club

```
          we there              shoulders & flies opening
       to make-believe          like Lost Boys scooping air
        & calling it cake       pulling apart chicken leg air
           with their teeth          it took me time
      to know the feelings I have      for boys on bikes
       with their tops off      sun slapping their chests
       are different from other girls'     the masc next to me
   says    think of niagara falls      in a newly testosteroned voice
      innocent cadence          yoyoing the walls
    the only water I think of              the sea        in my head
           it's way too special          to be piss
      my legs hover over the urinal              I was never
      comparing myself to other girls      because I wasn't one
         not because of confidence          I jut out my jaw
    in the mirror daily        & study the shapes boys make in a room
      in the club the drag king is pulling spaghetti from his crotch
I clutch the cardboard tube to mine        think of the Lost Boys' magic
         relieve myself        if the hand is no longer a hand
       when it takes hold of the hammer          my pussy
               is no longer
```

Jaime Lock

P. Hodges Adams is a poet from Michigan, USA. Their work has appeared or is forthcoming in *Shenandoah, Cutbank, Sycamore Review, New Orleans Review, December Magazine, Arkansas International, Northwest Review,* and elsewhere. They were a finalist for the 2022 Jeff Marks Memorial Poetry Prize, the 2021 *Connecticut River Review* experimental poetry prize, and the 2020 Graybeal-Gowen Prize for Virginia, USA writers.

Instagram: @thelastadams

Twitter: @thelastadams

types of woman i could have been

beheading dolls

                               needle-mouthed   the first novelist

        nymph

           slut

siren   or one who finds a man - one man -

                            marries him, lets him inside

        hair to my waist

                      bruised toes and perfect posture

your little wife, i

      clean the stove with vinegar

                      dress in black velvet, loan

              my eyes, my hands, my mouth,

          my body

                          nurse the doll back to health

      take in my own hems

                  swallow smoke without coughing

            let you pry up my pupils

                here for the music and the sex, i

                    give in, wrists first

i never cook with butter i never

    wear my shoes inside i never ask

        to stay the night

                or at least i'm gone by morning

   if i name a few stars on the walk home,

                that belongs to me

growing dill in my garden

                            illuminatrix with teeth of lapis lazuli

   or a warrior's wife, laying back in furs

      dead in childbirth

                sawed in half

        speakeasy gin

           undressed with the blocks of my body

             set down in oil paint

or would i always have been like this:
        joan-legacied
              shakespeare in reverse
     cutting my hair, speaking low?

sometimes i get this desire
    for you to touch me again
                like wishing for my own birth
            if only i could stomach it

P. Hodges Adams

David McGovern is a queer artist and educator from rural Ireland. He works with moving image, audio, performance, and text to create space for self-enquiry, reflection, and speculation. He is currently developing HARDCARE, a participatory artwork exploring unconventional and deviant care experiences. David received the Irish Arts Council's Next Generation Artist Award in 2022. His poetry has been published in *The Stinging Fly*.

Instagram: @davidm.govern

Twitter: @davidm_govern

The Bath Salts

Thank u 4 the bath salts.
I'll never use them.

I will however launch Grindr
On a flat afternoon in late November.
I'll do it because it activates a different part of me. It feels urgent,
                                              fizzing with suspense.

Having sex – the sex – it's fine – it's great

But the flirtation, and the levity, and the decision
to defy routine on a Thursday afternoon – that's the resistance.
                                              I fuck the clock.

                    I'm not at the hospital
                    I'm here

          I'm not at the hospital
          I'm here

I'm here. The door opens.
Two strangers.
I step inside.
Our heads are light, maybe.
Intimate.
Caring – fleetingly.

'They don't care, they just want one thing.'

Sure.

But I want many things, and
                    I get some of them here.
          I want to place pressure on their bare shoulders.

I want to not drink coffee and be polite.
I want to be wanted, despite the fall.
I want to be a fragment of me, a body.
I want to not explain and give no context.
I want to release and have a day unlike the others.

I arrive, not knowing much about them
(I'll delete them later)
but I'm here, I brought myself here
In that moment, on that flat afternoon
                          I inject care into the scene.

David McGovern

Niven Govinden is a writer from the UK who has written six acclaimed novels: *We Are The New Romantics* (2004), *Graffiti My Soul* (2007), *Black Bread White Beer* (2012), *All The Days and Nights* (2014), *This Brutal House* (2019), and *Diary of a Film* (2021). His work has been shortlisted for the Green Carnation Prize, the Polari Prize, the Gordon Burn Prize, and the DSC Prize for South Asian Literature.

Instagram: @niven_govinden

Twitter: @nivengovinden

50

It's not as easy as saying that
you can choose your family: those
you desire have to want
to be chosen.
Maybe you picked badly,
chasing those who could not
be constrained. As a kid,
your cheek was marked by a kitten
who took against you.
It's not a memory you retain –
you were a baby, but
perhaps there was a deficiency
even then: the scab
on your skin afterwards, coarse
and thick. Forming a barrier
that shielded the love
you longed to give;
that repelled the love
you long to receive.

Niven Govinden

Michael McKimm is an Irish writer living in London, UK. He is the author of the poetry collections *Still This Need* (Heaventree, 2009) and *Fossil Sunshine* (Worple, 2013), and has edited two anthologies: *MAP* (Worple, 2015) and *The Tree Line* (Worple, 2017). His poems appear in a number of anthologies, including *The Future Always Makes Me So Thirsty: New Poets from the North of Ireland* (Blackstaff, 2016) and *Queering the Green: Post-2000 Queer Irish Poetry* (Lifeboat Press, 2021). Michael's new collection *Because we could not dance at the wedding* will be published by Worple Press in 2023.

Twitter: @michaelmckimm

Aubade

Sometimes when we wake
and stir and turn and sleep again
rolled up like a carpet

there will be a rhythm coming
through the deep:
the tapping of your toe upon

the curled back of my feet.
A tapping I will waken to a code
with a dozed hand

that's reached across your chest
by matching with my thumb
your dancing, dreamy notes.

So you'll beat then a tap tap tap
like a woodpecker would
on my sole's gnarled wood

which I mimic in our practised way
before I play across your front
a tappity bodhrán flick

which your toes kick out quick.
No matter how long we've improvised
this irregular, attuned

surprise, this gentle sesh, this jam
I never know what rhyme you'll send
what restless telegram to say

are you now ready for the day?

Michael McKimm

Jesse Ogbeide is a poet from Nigeria. His work has been published in *Brittle Paper, Sledgehammer Lit,* and *open work* magazine.

Twitter: @ogbeidejess

Instagram: @ogbeidejesse

watching men walk from the library window, thinking about love

overwhelmed, I watch them
march through the spiny leaves,
the black ants: men sauntering
with the tiniest measure
across the field of green.
one of them drops his key.
he jumps, without hesitation,
into the darkness,
a ditch to another world;
I am more than I am.
it is the same: the men, the ants,
the body, and everything in it.
how eager they are
to dive, out of love,
into the mess of things.
how tender it can be
to stay: to watch,
even as the heart eats itself.

Jesse Ogbeide

SK Grout (she/they) is a writer, editor, and poet from Aotearoa New Zealand, who splits her time between London, UK, and Auckland Tāmaki Makaurau. Her debut pamphlet *What love would smell like*, is published with V. Press. She is a Feedback Editor for Tinderbox Poetry. Their poetry and reviews are widely published in the US, UK, Europe, and the Pacific, including in *Glass*, *Cordite Poetry Review*, *Magma Poetry*, *Finished Creatures*, and *Poetry Wales*. They won first prize in the Open Category at the 2022 Oxford Brookes International Poetry Competition.

For more information, visit skgroutpoetry.wixsite.com/poetry

Instagram: @indeskidge

Twitter: @indeskidge

The Hug

after Thom Gunn

End of term, we had drunk
ourselves silly on Spanish sherry
and flaming Jägerbombs.
Someone had produced a spliff
but it was only you and I who
sucked the life from it. Later,
I woke to feel you pressed
against me – the first surprise
your fingers pincered
round my wrist. When waking
thoughts rushed in, I felt
the soft cup of your breasts
imprinted upon my backbone
your left hip to my right
angle veering from the divine.
This was not sex, nor love,
nor even mild comfort.
It was waking into something
neither of us acknowledged
in our scheduled bodies:
that we wanted to feel
security stamped into embrace
that we were lonely, not alone.

SK Grout

Nour Kamel is a writer, editor, and baker from Cairo, Egypt. Their chapbook *Noon* is part of the New-Generation African Poets series and their work has been published in the *Shade Journal*, *just femme & dandy*, *World Literature Today*, and *Anomaly*, among other print and online journals.

Instagram/Twitter: @screamlnour

Michael Jacket

Every portrait you took of me was love   both, neither   of us
would admit until   wounds,   years later.
Mama had a jacket from the 80s   paired white hi-tops in a photo
Baba took,   her puckered mouth beginning to protest   food in hand
body in jacket,   their bodies made me   love me
despite   the willful unknowing.   You loved me,
made me too. Remember   all the moments
you painted   image after image after garment   of me,
of dressup,   of baby queers   in men's clothing   shoes shooing
lovely in kitsch leather   inherited   fear too   from Mama.
You both, my love,   would throw out separate parts of me   faded
with boyname stitched in   worn so often   worn adored in portraits
of me
you only took
and we both knew love   was each picture you took of me.

Nour Kamel

Lara Mae Simpson is a poet and writer from North Yorkshire, UK currently based in London, where they study at King's College London. Their work has been published by *Young Poets Network*, *Free Verse Revolution*, and *Pomegranate Magazine*. Lara is also a writer for the London-based arts and culture journal *Strand Magazine*.

Instagram: @laramaewrites

Twitter: @laramaesimpson

Portrait of My Lover as a Leather Jacket

after Selima Hill

Cold teeth trim my flesh clean—
you like to bite, like your zips
licking dresses underneath,
strawberry slicing into biker
fantasy, lion tail buckle hanging
from your hard waist sewn
with the smallest seams.
Your stitching is starting to fray.
Who knows how much blood
you patch up to gleam
in photographs, your pockets
chiaroscuro-heavy. Let me
take those phantom screams
& place them in my mouth, a screen.

Lara Mae Simpson

Amy Acre is a poet and freelance writer, and the editor of Bad Betty Press. Her pamphlets *And They Are Covered in Gold Light* (Bad Betty, 2019) and *Where We're Going, We Don't Need Roads* (flipped eye, 2015) were each chosen as a Poetry Book Society Pamphlet Choice. Her poem 'every girl knows' won the 2019 Verve Poetry Competition. She has written for Radio 4 and been featured on The Last Dinosaur's 2020 track, 'In the Belly of a Whale'. Her debut collection, *Mothersong*, will be published by Bloomsbury in September 2023. Amy was born and raised in London, and lives in Nottingham.

Instagram: @amyacre

Twitter: @amyacrepoet

Dance on My Grave
After Aidan Chambers

In St Mary's Garden,
my child is jumping on graves.
I try to catch her, unruly
pigeon, winging between
broken sundial, benches
that remember. She wants
me to dance with her
among the dogs and tilia,
stone chests and hart's-
tongue and I try to explain,
someone's under there.

A character actor
I can't place pretends
not to see us. I keep my eyes
on the slabs. Kid kicks
in tap, tails and top
hat holding a leaf, knows,
without knowing,
how rationed sunlight
—death's withholding—
makes us want
to turn up the bass.

Dance on My Grave was
a book I stole from school.
Library plastic-wrapped
thrill about two boys:
Southend geeks who held
each other from the ground
up. One, uprooted,
kept holding, while
the other became earth,

swallowing still
in the flower of grief

and as I read, I plunged
my tips into dirt, downing
fistfuls of queer and
glowing language,
rose and petaled,
my Cyberdog-dyed head
a many-coloured
baptisia spread, inhaled,
and concealed between
pages. Time capsule
to raise later.

There's nothing quiet
about the dead. Nitrogen
ghosts fibrillate soil into
spring that births birdsong.
Coral bells are bursting,
budding or spent and
I think of pissing in bushes,
the way bark feels
against your bare back,
dark yards haunted
by lighters and cider.

Child of mine sways,
resurrects a chorus
line of vertebrae.
I cave, rest on the
unwritten corner
of a ledger stone,
I'm sure they won't mind,
and keen for the thunder
if I were to rise in rhythm,

lift a boot and slam
it down, feel the dirt
give me back.

Amy Acre

JP Seabright is a queer disabled writer living in London. They have two solo pamphlets published, *Fragments from Before the Fall* (Beir Bua Press, 2021) and *No Holds Barred* (Lupercalia Press, 2022); and the collaborative works *GenderFux* (Nine Pens Press, 2022), which was shortlisted for a Saboteur Award, and *MACHINATIONS* (Trickhouse Press, 2022). They explore themes of gender, sexuality, trauma, and the climate crisis in their work spanning poetry, prose, experimental and audio/visual pieces. Links to this work and more information at jpseabright.com

Instagram: @jpseabright

Twitter: @errormessage

split/ting

i split my lip
  sweet stab of pain
taste of blood
  reminds me of the last time
with you
  as I lie under
Lempicka's *The Sleeper*
  desiring anything
but sleep
  the way you curved
your palm under
  my buttocks
cupping me
  holding on
owning me

i run my tongue
  along the cut
savouring warm hurt
  remembering us
fucking in filthy attic rooms
  mattress on the floor
in hotel bathrooms
  biting your hand
impaled against the door

thrown onto streets
  a gang of boys
threw stones at us
  called us names
one rock hit your neck
  i chased him
caught him
  fist drawn back
ready to strike

until he spits at me
his saliva spunking my lips

like yours had that morning
   as we climbed over
each other into the day
   dawn breaking upon
our sweat-slicked limbs

you split me
   into a person wanted
for the first time
   with a wound
so easily
   reopened

JP Seabright

Toby Buckley is an archivist and writer from Donegal, Ireland currently based in Belfast, where he studied Creative Writing (Poetry) at the Seamus Heaney Centre, Queen's University Belfast, and was the first recipient of the Ruth West Poetry Award Scholarship. Toby's poems have been published widely, including in *Poetry Ireland Review*, *The Stinging Fly*, *Empty House* (an anthology from Doire Press, 2021), and *Queering the Green* (Lifeboat Press, 2021). His first pamphlet, *Milk Snake*, was published by the Emma Press in 2022.

Instagram/Twitter: @longbeelad

Baby's Rosemary

Your mother rocks you with grief and relief
in equal measures, averting her gaze,
stealing furtive peeks in spite of herself
to seek a morsel of her genes in yours.
You are not the son she always wanted.
The coven pass her a cup of Lipton's
to smooth the shock of your body's wrongness
and distract her from their incantations.

Picture you, years from now, in the kitchen:
you all ankles and knees and baby teeth,
her back to her frocks and homemaker's vim.
Tell me she won't smile when you clatter in,
gracelessly skittering on cloven feet
across the lino like a fat spring lamb.

Toby Buckley

Tom Bland is a poet based in London, UK. He has two books published: the novel *Camp Fear* (Bad Betty, 2021), which was longlisted for the Polari First Book Prize, and *The Death of a Clown* (Bad Betty, 2018). He studied experimental theatre focusing on magical ritual in the arts.

Lucifer

solitude was its own demon   i sealed duct tape over my mouth
and nose
sitting
inside a large latex industrial waste bag
that formed a pyramid shape   over
my lotus position   the bag wrapped around my feet and buttocks
i felt the fear
of death   overcoming any sense of death   *but* death was there
        every brain was green   i knew this wasn't true but it didn't matter
        the image of green was stuck in my brain
the apocalypse had been predicted so many times   it hurt my
sense of dissolution to see
out of the window   the world was still here   not a burnt-out shell
with only mutating
flowers growing out of the cracks   into the atmosphere of acid rain
        the photograph had something to say   it was a
        picture of a family   not mine   but it
        reminded me of them   full of sad faces
        unable to speak or think together
like the ouroboros   i curled into a foetus
        inside this cocoon   lucifer was melting me from the inside out
        only desire was left   in its own fire
the wounds were love   but i couldn't say how this was so
        i felt giant hands holding me   all those eyes   all those faces
        out of the chaos
        lucifer was looking at me   face to face   he was so beautiful
        with glittering wings
        seeing the chaos i was falling through   *i was*   the tears
        the mouth   the scream   the ritual
        lucifer was in my blood
this poem was in my hands   the ill-conceived handwritten letters had
morphed together into   a mass of coiled lines   his sigil in front of me
        that pain surging along my spine
        all the heavy duty padlocks that fixed my vertebrae

into place   broke   broke   broke   broke   broke
broke   broke
broke   broke   broke   and i was holding myself so tight
i might have broken
my bones   but my iphone made a sound
      can you see the light of venus tonight xxx

Tom Bland